How to Enhance Your Storytelling with Music

Create Engaging and Memorable Storytelling for your Audience

Abimbola Gbemi Alao

"Music ... is the communicating link between the screen and the audience, reaching out and enveloping all into one single experience."

Bernard Herrmann

ISBN: 978-0-954625535

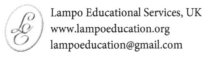 Lampo Educational Services, UK
www.lampoeducation.org
lampoeducation@gmail.com

"Anyone who has seen her perform will know that Abimbola is a magical storyteller. Her use of music and rhythm enhances and livens the stories and has a wonderful effect on her audiences. In this book she generously shares some of her secrets and opens up the world of music to other storytellers so that they too can have a share of the magic."

Alison Gagg (Education Manager Buckfast Abbey)

"This is certainly a very useful and practical guide and will encourage storytellers to try out new techniques regarding call-and-response/ use of music and song."

David Heathfield (Storyteller and University Lecturer)

"Having had the joy of witnessing Abimbola's storytelling sessions first-hand, I was excited to read her tips and strategies for incorporating music into sessions, and I wasn't disappointed. This is a practical, step-by-step resource that offers a treasure trove of advice and options for even the least confident musicians among us. I would highly recommend it for anyone who is seeking a fresh and engaging approach to storytelling."

Anna Payne (Year 1 Class Teacher, Abbey School)

"This useful book offers practical examples on how to add music and singing to performance storytelling. The tales demonstrate how songs can enhance stories and also give an audience the opportunity to be creative. Teachers and storytellers will be encouraged to use these tips."

Amy Robinson (Writer, Storyteller and Ventriloquist)

"This book will serve as an extremely helpful and inspiring guide for those who are new to musical improvisation in storytelling. It can be used as a tool for developing creative writing, and it is also beneficial for people who are looking for different approaches to enhance language and communication skills in a range of settings, from early years education to therapeutic intervention."

Kitty Heardman (English Language and Music Educator)

This brilliant book is a cross-curricula resource for teachers and storytellers. The information is refreshing and practical. Teachers who wish to create a magical experience in the classroom will find the practical information useful."

Grace Yesufu (Assistant Head Teacher, English and Literacy, The John Warner School)

"Abi has revived my passion for stories and equipped me with a range of new and innovative strategies to deliver/facilitate storytelling within the classroom and beyond."

Debbie Burman (English Deputy Manager, Stoke Damerel Community College)

"I have had the pleasure of working with Abi to co-teach trainee teachers at the University of St Mark & St John. Abi is an engaging storyteller and she inspires her students. There are useful ideas in this book for teachers who wish to explore storytelling in their classrooms. It is a great resource."

Susan Porter (Senior Lecturer, Department of Education, University of St Mark & St John)

Table of Contents

Introduction

It was a sunny Saturday afternoon and the book event I had been invited to was heaving with stalls containing books of every shape and size. I had arrived early enough to set up in a lovely room allocated for storytelling. I had been preparing for this event for weeks and was looking forward to an unforgettable time travel into the world of my tales with parents and their children.

Soon it was storytelling time and people started filing into the room. It wasn't one of those formal storytelling events with a compere to welcome people and introduce me, so I had to do both jobs. I greeted everyone and told them to look under their chairs, where I had placed various musical instruments: drums, shakers and bells. They all checked out their instruments and I could see that they were ready to go.

I told them where my story originated from, which was Russia, and announced that I was doing an African adaptation of the story entitled, 'The Dog and the Wolf'. I then asked the audience to pick up their instruments and taught them a simple rhythm to accompany the song that we were using for call-and-response storytelling. In this type of storytelling, the narrator starts a song or chant (this is the call) and the audience sings the chorus, thereby responding.

It was thrilling to watch the camaraderie amongst the people. Some were making fun of themselves as they struggled with their shakers and bells, and others were helping the little ones to hold or play their instruments properly. After the singing and the drumming had finished, I began my story.

Agogo

As I moved and glided around the people, we sang, clapped and played instruments together. The very young ones were particularly joyful and attentive. To my amazement, when I had finished the first session and ushered in another group, I saw a handful of people who had been in the first group come back for a second, and then a third time. It was a glorious and memorable day of storytelling with music, and there were more surprises in store. The organisers were so excited and impressed by the feedback they received from the participants that they booked me for the next event there and then.

I have been telling stories professionally in various settings for almost two decades. However, my best experiences have always coincided with the times I have used music in my storytelling. Music creates an unforgettable experience that helps me connect to my audience and get more storytelling and teaching opportunities. I have never taken out an advertisement in any magazine or newspaper, but word about my work gets around.

My journey has not always been this successful. Many years ago, having struggled to get a break in my storytelling career, I was on the verge of giving up. Thankfully, through enlivening my performances with music and rhythm, I managed to turn things around and the rest, as they say, is history.

The Aim of This Book

This book is a resource for storytellers, teachers and community workers who wish to create an engaging storytelling experience and connect more effectively with their audience. Parents and carers can also benefit from these ideas, even if they do not tell stories professionally. Every audience, whether they are in a theatre, classroom, community setting or at home, needs a good storyteller. You can make your storytelling memorable by implementing the ideas shared in this book.

I teach oral tradition skills to storytellers, trainee teachers, outdoor education practitioners and parents. One of the sessions I lead is how to use music to enhance storytelling. In this book, I have put together some of the ideas that I share with my students. This resource will be useful for practitioners or story lovers who have started telling stories and want to make their sessions lively.

In today's 'fast-paced' world, an audience will have been exposed to first-rate entertainment through films, theatre or television, so it may take more than straightforward narration to hold their attention. A storyteller needs to draw the audience into the world of their story. Some of the ways to do this successfully include:

1. Good preparation.

2. An appropriate and engaging story.

3. Creative use of the voice, i.e., pitch, pace, volume and quality.

4. Animated and expressive body language.

5. Using music to bring storytelling alive.

In this book, I will explore the last point in the list above. I intend to focus on West African storytelling because in that culture, call-and-response is a prominent style.

Tambourines

Why Music?

Music is a universal language that everyone connects with, irrespective of age, culture or race. Neurologist Petr Janata of the University of California says: "Music is a way of synchronizing groups of people and engaging in a common activity that everyone can do at the same time"[1]. I grew up in West Africa, where the oral tradition thrives. The method of narration predominantly used is known as call-and-response, whereby a live audience actively engages with the narrator. This makes the storytelling experience enriching and unforgettable.

One of the ways to create such an engaging experience is through music. Songs can be used to stir the emotion of an audience, thereby creating a high level of rapport between the teller and the listener. In my experience, the audience, even those who are unfamiliar with this style, are always curious about call and response storytelling. They find learning a new song, especially in a foreign language, exciting, and they enjoy the challenge. They love being part of the narrative journey – singing, learning and playing together.

---

[1] NIH News in Health (2010) Strike a chord for health: Music matters for body and mind
Available from: http://newsinhealth.nih.gov/2010/January/feature1.htm. [Accessed: May 2015]

A few years ago at a storytelling event in Plymouth, a journalist from BBC Radio Devon interviewed me and asked why I was so passionate about the oral tradition and what makes a successful storytelling event. My answer to the former was long, but the response I gave to the second question is more relevant to this book.

I told the journalist that storytelling is successful when it is memorable. My hope is that my audiences remember our time together, think about the experience we enjoyed and continue to pass on the stories and songs that I shared with them.

I'll tell you a story that illustrates this further. One day, I visited a primary school in Cornwall. One of the teachers came to the staff room, where I was getting my musical instruments ready for the day, and said that some children were standing by the door and wanted to see me. I opened the door to find a group of 6 to 7 year old students. They started singing '*Kulumbu Yeye*', one of the songs that I had taught them about 2 years previously!

How does music enhance storytelling?

1. It helps create a memorable experience. When music is used in storytelling, people are better able to remember the narrative and its central message.

2. It helps to set the mood for your storytelling. Therefore, it is important to choose the right music for the mood of the narrative: scary, happy, mysterious…

3. It keeps the audience engaged and alert. Your listeners want to get it right, so they listen attentively, especially

to the cue that tells them when to start singing. This means the audience will not be easily distracted.

4. It gives a sense of satisfaction. The audience feel that they have been part of the whole narrative experience. A sense of 'community' is built as the emphasis shifts from 'you' as the storyteller to 'us' having a storytelling experience.

What are the practical ways of using music in storytelling?

There are a few ways to use music in storytelling, but the three that I use mostly are:

1. Direct call-and-response singing

2. CDs or downloaded music

3. Musical improvisation

Castanets

Part One

Direct Call and Response Singing:
How to Use Songs or Rhythms in Storytelling

Preparation

Call-and-response narration needs some preparation before the storytelling event. Firstly, the storyteller will need to learn the song that she plans to use and rehearse it with the rhythm she intends to play on the percussion: bells, drums, shakers, or any other musical instrument. Thanks to the Internet, songs and rhythms are more accessible now than they were many years ago. I have a repertoire of Yoruba songs that I use with my stories; I teach some of them during workshops and I've also made some available for easy download. However, when I'm telling stories from other cultures, I spend time learning the songs or rhythms that I intend to use; this gives me the confidence to perform well.

Getting Started

The first thing to do when standing in front of an audience is to introduce yourself and let them key into your voice before you start the performance. This is crucial, especially if there is no compere to introduce you. Even if you've been introduced, it is still polite to 'warm up' to the audience with whom you'll be sharing stories. Here is one of the ways I do this:

Hello everyone, my name is Abimbola and I am here to tell you a story. How are you all?

As I say this, I smile, make eye contact with the audience, and pause to listen to their comments before I continue:

Today, I would like to take you on a journey to a far away land, but before we set off, I want to teach you the song that we are going to sing as we travel. Are you ready?

At this point, I may sit down and play a simple rhythm on a djembe drum or shaker, just to calm everyone down and get them totally focused on me. Some people will sway or nod to the rhythm as they eagerly await the next exciting part.

Sometimes, once I have everyone's attention, I decide to sing a popular song or rhyme, depending on the age group. A few of the songs that I use are available for download online:

You can listen to or download the song from:
www.storytellerabi.bandcamp.com

I also sometimes teach the audience a clap rhythm or body movement. One of the benefits of this action-packed storytelling is that everyone wants to get it right, so they listen attentively to know what to do and when to do it.

I always teach a song or chant before I start my story so that the telling will be smooth and effective. I try to use short verses that can be repeated as many times as I want because long ones may take a while to learn, and they may hinder the audience from enjoying the narrative. After practising the song two or three times, I may say the following before I begin my story:

You learnt that song so quickly, well done! Now, are you sitting comfortably? Then I shall begin.

'Once upon a time...'

Incorporating Song into the Story

Below is a short story titled 'The Dancing Dog and the Leopard'. It is my West African adaptation of the short story entitled, 'The Chihuahua and the Leopard'. I heard the story at a conference many years ago and despite searching for its source or author, I have been unable to find any information on it. I love telling the story because I'm passionate about trickster tales, which is why I wrote an adaptation of it a few years ago. In the story, the points where the storyteller brings in the song are highlighted in italics. You can practise it with your group and enjoy seeing the narration unfold!

Story:
The Dancing Dog and the Leopard

(A West African adaptation of The Chihuahua and the Leopard)

Once upon a time, in the animal village of Jago, there was a dog called Aja. He was a natural bobtail with a special talent – he was an excellent dancer! At that time, no one had ever seen a dancing dog so the news of Aja's special skill travelled throughout the land.

Aja only danced to one song that his mother had taught him when he was a tiny puppy. His mother told him the importance of going to school. She said: "My son, if you learn how to read and write, the world is your oyster; you can learn new skills and make money to buy nice shoes, not just the cheap ones that many of us wear."

"But Mama," Aja replied, "The other animals will laugh at me when I go to school - I have no tail!"

"You are a very special dog with a great talent, you must always remember that," his mother assured him. Unfortunately, Aja's mother died before he was old enough to go to school, but Aja did not forget the song she had taught him. He sang it every day until the entire village learnt it and many animals sang it. Each time Aja heard his favourite song, he jumped up and performed amazing dance moves that made him very famous.

Many animals came from far and near to watch the dancing dog, and he gave his audience good value for their time. The song became well-known in the entire region because it was the only song that inspired Aja to entertain with his amazing dance. The song is called *Bata:*

Storyteller and audience sing Bata in a call and response style.

Call:	*Bata re a dun ko ko ka*
Response:	*Bata re a dun ko ko ka*
Call:	*Bi o ba kawe re*
Response:	*Bata re a dun ko ko ka*
Call:	*Bata re a wo serere nile*
Response:	*Bata re a wo serere nile*
Call:	*Bo o ba kawe re*
Response:	*Bata re a wo serere nile*

Translation

Call:	*You shall wear expensive shoes*
Response:	*You shall wear expensive shoes*
Call:	*If you work hard at school*
Response:	*You shall wear expensive shoes*
Call:	*You will wear cheap shoes*
Response:	*You will wear cheap shoes*
Call:	*If you do not work hard at school*
Response:	*You will wear cheap shoes*

**You can listen to or download the song from:
https://storytellerabi.bandcamp.com/track/ko-ko-
ka-african-playground-music**

The genet, a solitary animal who did not like Aja's fanfare, was not happy about his popularity. "Hmm… some animals dance around like fools while some of us work hard, hunting for food to feed our families. Everywhere you go, Aja this, Aja that; one day he'll dance himself to his grave," he moaned bitterly.

One day, Aja's village hosted the annual yam festival and all the animals came to Jago village. There were drummers and singers from every region and Aja, as usual, was the life and soul of the show. Everyone began to sing Aja's favourite song – *Bata*:

Storyteller and audience sing Bata

Call:	*Bata re a dun ko ko ka*
Response:	*Bata re a dun ko ko ka*

16

Call:	*Bi o ba kawe re*
Response:	*Bata re a dun ko ko ka*
Call:	*Bata re a wo serere nile*
Response:	*Bata re a wo serere nile*
Call:	*Bo o ba kawe re*
Response:	*Bata re a wo serere nile*

Aja leapt and twirled, dancing his soul out. He became so engrossed in his dance that he did not realise he had begun to move away from the crowd and into the forest. The rhythm of the drums continued to echo, *dum dum dum gundun dum*, deep within his soul, and with closed eyes he continued to dance, thinking he was still with the crowd. He soon realised that the sound of drumming was fading and he shouted, "please don't stop, louder; louder!" But the sound became more distant. He stopped dancing, looked around and barked, "I said louder!" Then he realised there wasn't a single animal in sight.

"Oh no! Where am I?" he cried.

Aja had wandered far away from home into the jungle, and he was lost. He tried to find his way out of the forest, but in spite of all his efforts he seemed to be going deeper and deeper into the jungle.

Soon, he saw a hungry looking leopard moving stealthily towards him and he knew he was in trouble. He quickly came up with an idea – *dance for him...? No! Such a move would only make me a more attractive meal for the beast*, he thought.

Meanwhile, the genet was sitting on a tree above, watching with keen interest at the event unfolding down below. He was excited that at last his enemy was going to get what he deserved.

The dog remembered the words of his late mother. When you are in trouble, PAUSE, TAKE A DEEP BREATH, PRAY AND THINK!

As the leopard edged in closer, the dog looked around and noticed some fresh bones on the ground. He began to chew on them, pretending he hadn't noticed the leopard. As the big animal was about to leap, Aja smacked his lips and exclaimed loudly, "Wow, that was one delicious leopard. I wonder if there are any more around here?"

The leopard stopped mid-stride and gently backed away into the forest. "Phew," he said, "that was close - that evil little dog nearly ate me up."

The genet, who had seen everything, was furious and decided to knock some sense into the stupid leopard. Aja saw him as he went after the leopard and knew he was up to no good. The genet soon caught up with the leopard and told him everything he had seen, and how the dog had made a fool of him. The leopard was furious! He didn't want anyone, let alone a tiny dog, making a fool out of him. He offered the genet a ride back to where the dog was so that he could deal with him.

Aja saw them coming and feared the worst, but again, he quickly turned his back and pretended he hadn't seen them. When the leopard and genet were close enough, he shouted,

"Okay, so where's that genet that I sent to bring me another leopard? Why is he not here?"

At this point, depending on how much time I've got, I may pause and ask a question:
"What do you think happened to the genet?"

18

I would allow a couple of people to give us suggestions on what they think happened to the genet, before ending the story as follows:

The leopard stopped mid-stride, pulled the frightened genet off his back, and dragged him back into the forest. As for Aja the dancing dog … well, he eventually found his way out of the forest and he danced happily ever after.

Djembe Drums

Part Two

Using CDs or Downloaded Music to Enhance Storytelling

The second method that I'd like to focus on in this book is using CDs or downloaded music to enhance storytelling. This approach is easier than the first, as the storyteller does not have to learn a song or create a rhythm to go with it. They can simply play a song from a CD or music-playing device and use it during the narration.

One of the advantages of this style is that the storyteller can easily access music and ready-made rhythms from various cultures. This may be more convenient for storytellers who do not feel confident using hand percussion or musical instruments.

Personally, I use both methods successfully, but some storytellers say they prefer the immediacy of live music, as opposed to CDs. Some also say that they find the change of mode in the middle of the story distracting. I don't have an issue with this, perhaps because I have been doing it for a long time and have learnt to switch from story to song easily. Nevertheless, I would suggest that if a storyteller is doing this for the first time, she might play the music or song at the beginning and end of the story.

Preparation:

Unlike the 'direct call-and-response' singing, there isn't much preparation needed when using CDs or downloaded music. However, before the storytelling session, you may want to give the music to one of the organisers or a student and give them a cue for when the song should be played.

Getting Started

As earlier mentioned, the first thing to do when standing in front of an audience is to introduce yourself and let them key into your voice before you start the performance. This is crucial, especially if there is no compere to introduce you. Even if you've been introduced, it is still polite to 'warm up' to the audience with whom you'll be sharing stories. Here is one of the ways I do this:

Hello everyone, my name is Abimbola and I am here to tell you a story. How are you all?

As I say this, I smile, make eye contact with the audience, and pause to listen to their comments before I continue:

Today, I would like to tell you the story of 'The Tortoise and the Singing Drum'. How many people here have been naughty at one time or another?… Be honest now…

Okay, the story is about a boy whose disobedience got him into such serious trouble that he ended up in the tortoise's drum! Who's ready for the story?

At this point, I go straight into the story, because, unlike the method I use in 'direct call-and-response singing', I don't need to teach a song or rhythm.

Story:
The Tortoise and the Singing Drum

Once upon a time, there was a boy called Atilola. His parents loved him dearly because he was their only child and they made sure he wanted for nothing. They treated him like a delicate egg and would not allow anyone to reprimand him, even when he behaved very badly. Because of this, Atilola found it difficult to obey instructions.

One day, during the rainy season, Atilola, who was ten years old at the time, told his mother that he was going outside to play with his friends.

"Stay in the neighbourhood and do not wander off into the valley; the sky is heralding rain," warned his mother. But, as usual, Atilola ignored his mother's advice and ran off to find his friends.

"Let's go and look for honey in the beehive in Oyin valley," Atilola said to his friends once they had gathered together at the edge of the village. The boys agreed, and so they all set off on the four-mile journey in search of honey. As the boys approached Oyin, they noticed that the sky was beginning to turn grey. The first thunderclap made Atilola's friends panic. One boy stepped forward and said: "We should get back to our homes before the rain comes."

This was sensible advice and all the other boys, except Atilola, agreed to return home immediately.

"Not me!" yelled Atilola. "I have come here to find honey and I will not leave until I find some."

"But how can you find honey in the rain?" asked another boy.

"If I cannot find honey in the rain," said Atilola, "then I will stay right here until it stops raining!" And just as the words left his mouth, tiny drops of rain began to fall from the sky and tickled their bare backs.

Upon seeing the rain, the other boys scampered off in the direction of the village leaving Atilola to hunt for the honey alone. Before long, the little drops of rain formed a puddle and Atilola jumped around in it, splashing and dancing and waving his arms.

Some of the farmers returning from the fields saw Atilola dancing in the puddle and told him to go home, but the boy would not listen; instead, he wrinkled up his nose, stuck out his tongue and continued to dance in the puddle as the rain grew heavier and heavier.

Soon, the sky began to empty its contents in sheets and buckets, and the heavy downpour flooded the entire valley in no time at all. Atilola could not find a place to hide. He looked around until eventually he saw an Odan tree and hurried towards it. Just as he was about to climb the tree, he slipped and fell into the water and the floods quickly engulfed him. As the waters carried Atilola down through the valley towards the big river, he screamed and howled in fear of his life, but there was nobody around to hear the frightened boy.

He tried to reach out and grab hold of anything that might keep him afloat - twigs, logs, poles - but it was no use, he could not get a proper grip because he was moving too fast.

Then he saw a house in the distance and screamed at the top of his voice, hoping to gain the attention of those inside.

"Help!" he cried. "Please help me!"

Ijapa, the tortoise, heard the noise and opened his window to see what was happening. He was shocked to see a boy struggling to swim against the flood, so he hurried out of his house to help. The tortoise took a long pole from the shed in his front yard and stretched it out across the water towards the boy.

"Quick, grab a hold!" yelled Ijapa.

Atilola reached out for the pole and grabbed it with both hands, holding on tightly as Ijapa pulled him to safety. As soon as the boy was out of the water, Ijapa took him into the house, built a fire and served soup to warm Atiola up.

But Ijapa was not generous by nature; all the time he was busy deciding what he might gain from the unsuspecting boy.

This question was quickly answered after Atilola had drained his bowl of soup and curled up on a mat in a corner of the room. Before he drifted off to sleep, he began to sing in the most beautiful voice Ijapa had ever heard. It was a lullaby that Atilola's mother used to sing to him when he was a little boy.

Storyteller gives cue to the helper who plays the CD or downloaded music.

Song:

Call:	*Ojo maa ro ojo maa ro; itura lo je*
Response:	*Ojo maa ro ojo maa ro; itura lo je*
Call:	*Eweko o yo boo ba ro*
Response:	*Eweko o yo*
Call:	*Agbado o yo boo ba ro*
Response:	*Agbado o yo*
Call:	Emi o le leran lara boo ro
Response:	*Emi o ni yo kun*
Call:	*Ojo maa ro ojo maa ro itura lo je*
Response:	*Ojo maa ro ojo maa ro itura lo je*

Translation

Call:	*Rain please fall; you are refreshing*
Response:	*Rain please fall; you are refreshing*
Call:	*Plant can't grow if you don't fall*
Response:	*Plant can't grow*
Call:	*Corn can't grow if you don't fall*
Response:	*Corn can't grow*
Call:	*I won't be healthy if you don't fall*
Response:	*I won't be healthy*
Call:	*Rain please fall; you are refreshing*
Response:	*Rain please fall; you are refreshing*

You can listen to or download the song from:
https://storytellerabi.bandcamp.com/track/ojo-maa-
ro-african-playground-song

As the song is playing, I sway to the music and invite my audience to join me. This helps us connect with the song and enhances the musical experience; otherwise, everybody will listen to the song in silence. When the storyteller moves rhythmically to the song, the audience feels 'present' at the setting and enjoys the story more.

We also do rainfall actions. This involves lifting our hands as we dance and wiggling our fingers as we bring them back down, mimicking rainfall. We do this rhythmically, not just mechanically.

The storyteller may choose to play the song once or
twice, after which she continues the story...

Ijapa was mesmerised by the song, and as he swayed to the enchanting rhythm, a mischievous plan came into his head. He waited until the boy was fast asleep, then crept out of the house to his backyard, where he began to carve a big wooden drum.

He worked throughout the night until his task was complete, and when Atilola awoke the next morning, Ijapa asked him to hop inside the drum.

"Why do you want me to get inside the drum?" asked Atilola.

The tortoise smiled innocently and told the boy that he simply wanted to test the drum's sound. "It is not such a huge favour to ask, given that I saved you from the floods, is it?"

Atilola had to agree that he owed the tortoise a great debt for saving his life, and so he climbed inside the drum and the tortoise covered it over with stretched hide. He had already created small holes on the side of the wood so that the boy could breathe.

Once Atilola was hidden inside, Ijapa instructed him to sing the song 'Ojo maa ro' each time he hit the drum with a stick.

Meanwhile, Atilola's parents were waiting anxiously for their son to return home. He had been gone all night and his mother was beside herself with worry.

After the flood had subsided, they went into the valley in search of their son, but they could not find him anywhere. Eventually, they went to the palace to report Atilola missing. When the king heard the distressing news, he sent his servants to search the entire village and its environs. They too could not find the boy and eventually the search was abandoned.

Ijapa was unaware of all the commotion as he stood in the village square and shouted out to passers-by, "Come and listen to my singing drum! It is truly the most beautiful thing you will ever hear."

Many people gathered to witness the spectacle, and each time the tortoise banged on the drum with his stick, Atilola sang from within. All those who listened were enthralled by his beautiful voice. Many were so captivated by the singing drum that they threw their caps and headgear to the floor and danced until they could dance no more.

Nobody could see the boy trapped inside; they all thought it was a magical drum and so they gave the crafty tortoise a great deal of money for such entertainment. Word soon spread throughout the entire neighbourhood and everyone came to see Ijapa and his singing drum.

The following day, Ijapa was ordered to the palace, as the king was also very eager to listen to the magical singing drum. Ijapa was pleasantly surprised to see many people in the palace courtyard. The king had invited the entire village for the great entertainment, and there was not a single space left where one might sit.

The tortoise gained a great deal of confidence from the crowd and insisted that he be paid in gold before he played his drum. The king had never heard of such a request, but as he was so anxious to hear the drum, he handed over a bag of gold and commanded the tortoise to begin.

Beaming with relish, Ijapa quickly banged on his drum, and again the beautiful voice began to sing the song 'Ojo maa ro'.

Storyteller gives cue to the helper who plays the CD or downloaded music.

Song:

| Call: | *Ojo maa ro ojo maa ro; itura lo je* |
| Response: | *Ojo maa ro ojo maa ro; itura lo je* |

Call:	*Eweko o yo boo ba ro*
Response:	*Eweko o yo*
Call:	*Agbado o yo boo ba ro*
Response:	*Agbado o yo*
Call:	*Emi o le leran lara boo ro*
Response:	*Emi o ni yo kun*
Call:	*Ojo maa ro ojo maa ro itura lo je*
Response:	*Ojo maa ro ojo maa ro itura lo je*

The king, the chiefs and everyone in the palace courtyard immediately got up to dance. Despite such merriment and dancing, the king noticed a woman sitting in a corner. She was crying uncontrollably while her husband tried in vain to console her. The king stopped the entertainment immediately and ordered the couple to be brought before him. He was furious because it was taboo for anyone to cry in the presence of a monarch.

The woman bowed before the king and told him that Ijapa's drum was not magical at all; it was her son, Atilola, who was singing inside it, she was certain. "No mother could bear the thought of her only son being held prisoner in such a manner," she sobbed.

The king commanded his guards to tear off the hide from the top of the drum so that they might all see what was inside.

When the hide was finally removed, Atilola slowly stepped out of the drum, blinking against the bright sun but grateful to be free at last. When he saw his parents, he ran to hug them both with tears of joy in his eyes. The entire palace erupted into a terrible commotion, as many people were shocked that Ijapa would deceive them in such a way.

The king ordered his guards to lock Ijapa up in jail, but the crafty tortoise was quick to point out to the king that the flood would have killed the boy had he not rescued him from the waters by pulling him to safety.

The king thought long and hard about Ijapa's defence and eventually decided to set the tortoise free. But the wise king warned against such tricks in the future, and he also took back his bag of gold for good measure.

As for Atilola, he decided that it was wiser to listen to his mother more often and not to behave like such a spoilt child. And so it was that Atilola and his parents lived happily ever after.

Sekere

Part Three

Musical Improvisation

Musical improvisation has limitless potential to make any storytelling session a memorable experience. I enjoy using this method in preschools, adult learning centres, memory cafés and care homes. This is because when I work with very young children or adults with learning difficulties, I do not perform long narratives. My audiences are the storytellers and music becomes a crucial part of the narrative experience. How I discovered musical improvisation is an interesting story, so I'd like to share a brief version of it with you…

Many years ago, when I first started my storytelling performances, I expected everyone to sit quietly and only participate when they were invited. However, I soon learnt that in a classroom of 2 to 4 year olds, that isn't always the case. Whenever I got a phone call to work with toddlers, I was apprehensive because I didn't know how best to perform for preschool children.

One day, a head teacher in Cornwall invited me to the opening ceremony of her school's new nursery, and she wanted me to work with a group of toddlers. Usually I would politely decline, but I needed some work, so I reluctantly said yes and marked the date in my diary.

On the day of the event, the head teacher led me to the room where the children and their teachers were waiting, and introduced me to the group. I had prepared a short tale because of the age of the children. It was an exciting event for them and I doubted that they would sit quietly through a long narrative.

Not long into my story, the children began to fidget and one of them decided to walk around the room, sucking noisily on her dummy. She threw toys at the other children and some of them later joined her. The teachers began to apologise as they frantically tried to 'catch' the children and bring them back to their seats. My young audience thought the chaos was fun and ran around dodging their teachers. I sat there sheepishly thinking, *here we go, this is why I don't add nurseries to my client lists!* I had two options at that moment, sink or swim, and I chose the latter.

I got off my seat, picked up my djembe drum and walked around the room with the children, singing stories and rhymes. Soon, everyone joined me and we began to chant some good old nursery rhymes. After the merrymaking, I told the children to sit down and asked if anyone wanted to tell us a story. A 3-year-old girl shared her experience of coming to a new school. It was hilarious! I was astounded by her gesticulation, her vocabulary and the varied tones she used for different characters. A lively environment of singing and dancing is indeed an inspiring setting for creative storytelling.

I left the nursery that day a happy storyteller who had found a precious gem. That gem was how to use musical improvisation to enhance my storytelling with very young children. Since then, I have constantly tried to work on how to make my sessions more engaging.

In this session, I will focus on the two methods that I use successfully when working with young children.

1. Musical improvisation with questions to prompt storytelling:

When I work with toddlers, I use rhymes that link with the theme of the school's event or programme. I choose rhymes that tell stories instead of ones that focus solely on onomatopoeic sounds. An example is: 'Mary Had a Little Lamb'. This song is a brilliant story with a linear structure. Before we start the session, I give out percussion instruments to the group and we play together. The children are always excited by the variety of sounds coming from instruments such as: cowbells, djembe drums, kashishis, sekeres and castanets.

Sometimes, a natural rhythm emerges and I enhance it by using my drum. For example, if I want the sekeres to be louder, I'll move closer to the children playing them and raise the tempo of my own drum, just as a conductor would point her baton at a group in an orchestra. After having fun improvising on percussion instruments, I then introduce a rhyme that we can sing, and I ask questions. For example, if we sing 'Mary Had a Little Lamb', I may ask the following open-ended questions that usually encourage more storytelling:

- Who has a lamb on their farm and what is the name of your lamb?

- Why does Mary's lamb love her so much?

- Do you think Mary sings to her lamb?

- What name should we give Mary's lamb?

2. Musical improvisation interspersed with narratives:

This second method helps me to explore creative writing; hence I find it exciting and rewarding. Some rhymes inspire me to create short stories that can be incorporated into songs. An example of such is 'Twinkle, Twinkle, Little Star'. Below is a practical way by which I use this rhyme; I have written it in a dramatic form for your enjoyment:

Telling the Story of Twinkle, the Little Star

Storyteller: Hello children, I am going to tell you the story of a star called Twinkle, but this story is a song, so we will tell it together with dancing and singing. Are you ready?

Children: Yes…!

Storyteller: Who will help me do the actions?

Children: Me…!

Storyteller divides the group into two. Group 1 sings the call and group 2 responds. Storyteller also gives out percussion instruments, such as sekeres and castanets, to some of the older children. Then she starts to play the drum:

Group 1: Twinkle, twinkle, little star, how I wonder what you are!

Group 2: Up above the world so high, like a diamond in the sky.

Group 1: Twinkle, twinkle, little star, how I wonder what you are!

Storyteller: Wow! Well done everybody. Now who is ready to hear how Twinkle became a very bright star?

Children: Me…!

Storyteller: Okay, you can sit down now, but each time I say **Twinkle**, you will clench your fist and open it like this…

Storyteller shows children how to do the action for a shining star.

Storyteller: When I say **Cloudy**, pretend you are throwing a large blanket at someone, and when I say **Prince**, raise your shoulders and move them up and down like this…

Storyteller shows children what to do.

Storyteller: Are you ready?

Children: Yes…!

Storyteller: Once upon a time, there was a star called **Twinkle**. She was a very bright star, but an evil genie called **Cloudy** would not allow her to shine her light for the world. **Cloudy** threw a dark blanket over her and laughed. "Ha ha ha, no one will ever know you are a bright star like a diamond," he said.

Sadly, no one saw **Twinkle's** brightness and nobody knew what she really looked like. One day, a powerful **Prince** was passing by and he saw **Twinkle** trying to shine under the dark blanket. The **Prince** stopped to ask questions:

Prince: (Group 1 sings) Twinkle, twinkle, little star, how I wonder what you are!

Twinkle: (Group 2 sings) Up above the world so high, like a diamond in the sky.

Prince: (Group 1 sings) Twinkle, twinkle, little star, how I wonder what you are!

Storyteller: The prince looked at *Twinkle* closely and saw that indeed she was a star that shone like a diamond, but she was covered by *Cloudy's* dark blanket. He pulled the blanket off *Twinkle*. This made *Cloudy* angry and he tried to attack the Prince. The Prince fought and overcame *Cloudy,* and he told him never to cover *Twinkle* again. *Twinkle* was very happy and she continued to shine happily ever after.

If you go out tonight, you may still see *Twinkle* winking at you from the sky and shining ever so brightly.

Now let's sing together.

Storyteller and Children: (Storyteller plays the djembe or sekere and everyone sings) "Twinkle, twinkle, little star, how I wonder what you are! Up above the world so high, like a diamond in the sky. Twinkle, twinkle, little star, how I wonder what you are!"

In Part One and Part Two above, the emphasis is on stories and how music can be used to enhance them. I use this method when I work in schools, and at community events, churches and other storytelling occasions. However, the focus in Part Three is on musical improvisation and using music to tell a story. I often use this method when working with toddlers or pre-schoolers.

I am currently developing a programme for people living with dementia, which is based on the method in Part Three of this book. When I work with people who have memory problems, I rarely teach them rhythms. Instead, I encourage them to improvise and enjoy good music without the pressure of having to remember what they have done. They use their imagination to make music and tell stories spontaneously. One day, I hope to share the story of how to use musical improvisation to enhance storytelling for people living with dementia.

Kashishi

Conclusion

Using music to enhance storytelling is easier than you think. Unfortunately, many storytellers miss out on this brilliant experience. They think that because they are not professional singers or musicians, they shouldn't bother trying. You don't need to be a professional to sing a simple song or play a rhythm. Having said that, you could always find a local drumming or percussion group in which to learn a few rhythms.

Some storytellers who have tried the simple methods in this book find that they can actually play by ear, and are able to gently strum a Kora or create rhythms on a djembe or shaker, without going to any formal music school. Remember that there is also the option of using pre-recorded songs or music.

You don't need sophisticated musical instruments to implement the ideas in this book. Some of my students have used household materials to create fantastic rhythms. A few years ago, during a storytelling assessment for a group of trainee teachers, a student used a container filled with dry beans during her presentation. Another student told the story of 'The Tortoise and the Singing Drum' and gave us tins that had dry grains in them. She told us to shake them each time she described rainfall. We all had fun!

Many others have shared their experiences of using music to enhance their storytelling. One of my students who used to volunteer at a local children's club, started running storytelling sessions there. Her performances delighted the children and caught the attention of the organisers. They gave her a Saturday job in the same place, in order to continue doing the storytelling.

Also, a tutor who works freelance, teaching English as a Foreign Language (EFL) said she started getting more opportunities to teach during summer because her class was always lively with music and storytelling. Her students did well in their tests and many more wanted to work with her. Many EFL students come from oral cultures and they are used to learning through musical narratives, so it makes sense to create an atmosphere conducive to creative learning.

I encourage you to also give the ideas in this book a try in your next performance or workshop. Incorporate music into your storytelling, it will surely be an enriching experience for you and your audience.

I hope you enjoy using the ideas I've shared in this mini book. Please check out my book 'Trickster Tales *for* Telling' for more call-and-response stories.

Finally: Remember Etiquette

Always make sure you obtain full copyright from music owners before using or downloading songs. Look online to find out how you can use such materials. Some people will allow you to download their music for personal use only, while others will give permission for you to use it for public performances once you have paid a stipulated amount.

About the Author

Abiṃbola Gbeṃi Alao

Abimbola is an author, lecturer, performance storyteller and a children's book translator. Her work includes the Yoruba translation of: 'Hansel and Gretel', 'The Little Red Hen and the Grain of Wheat', and several other books published by Mantra Lingua. Abimbola is the author of 'The Legendary Weaver: New Edition', 'The Goshen Principle', and 'Trickster Tales for Telling'. She is an award-winning playwright and her short play, 'Legal Stuff', won the BBC/Royal Court 24 Degrees Competition in 2008. She is also the founder of 'Story-Weavers for Dementia', a programme that uses a non-pharmacological approach for dementia care, and she is the compiler of 'Narrative Adventures from Plymouth Memory Café'.

Other Books by Abimbola Gbemi Alao

The Goshen Principle: A Shelter in the Time of Storm
By Abimbola Gbemi Alao

ISBN
Paperback: 9780954625511
Ebook: 9780954625559

The Legendary Weaver: New Edition
By Abimbola Gbemi Alao

ISBN
9780954625528

Trickster Tales for Telling
By Abimbola Gbemi Alao

ISBN
9780954625542

Dual Language books, translated by Abimbola Gbemi Alao

Floppy's Friends:
'Awon ore e Floppy'
Dual Language Yoruba
translation by Abimbola Alao.
(2004) Mantra Lingua.

ISBN
1 84444240 3

Hansel and Gretel:
'Hansel ati Gretel'
Dual Language Yoruba
translation by Abimbola Alao.
(2005) Mantra Lingua.

ISBN
1 84444778 2

The little Red Hen and the
Grains of Wheat: 'Adie Pupa
Kekere ati Eso Alikama'
Dual Language Yoruba
translation by Abimbola Alao.
(2005) Mantra Lingua.

ISBN
1 84444219 5

Nita Goes to Hospital:
'Nita lo si ile iwosan'
Dual Language Yoruba
translation by Abimbola Alao.
(2005) Mantra Lingua.

ISBN
1 84444836 3

Grandma's Saturday Soup:
'Obe Ojo Abameta Mama Agba'
Dual Language Yoruba
translation by Abimbola Alao.
(2005) Mantra Lingua.

ISBN
1 84444951 3

Welcome to the world baby:
'Kaabo sinu aye Omo titun'
Dual Language Yoruba
translation by Abimbola Alao.
(2005) Mantra Lingua.

ISBN
1 84444297 7

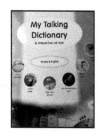

My Talking Dictionary &
Interactive CD ROM
Yoruba & English – Yoruba
translation by Abimbola Alao.
(2005) Mantra Lingua.

ISBN
1 84444717 0

Lightning Source UK Ltd.
Milton Keynes UK
UKHW02f2116010818
326640UK00012B/451/P